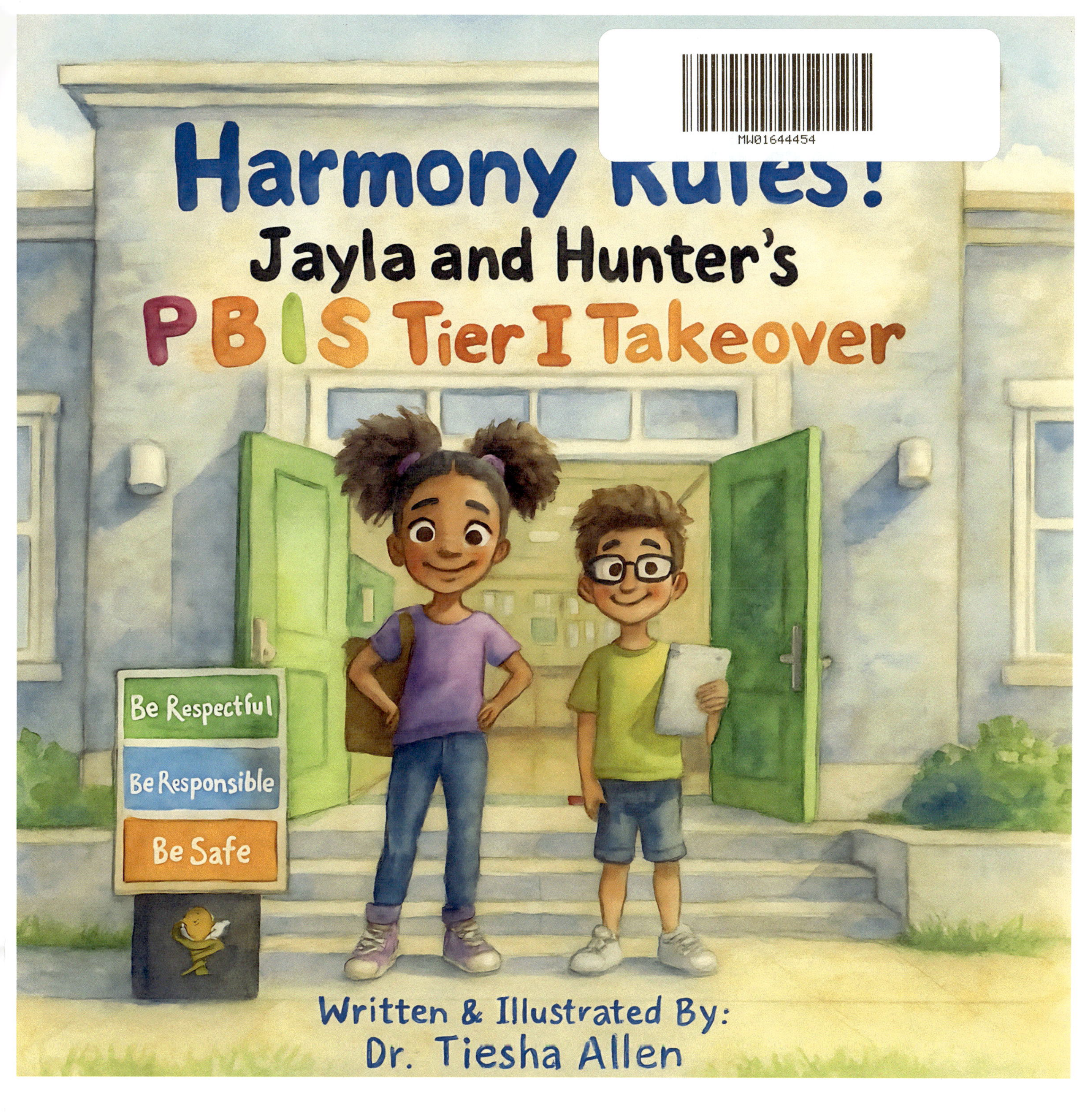
Harmony Rules!
Jayla and Hunter's
PBIS Tier I Takeover
Be Respectful
Be Responsible
Be Safe
Written & Illustrated By:
Dr. Tiesha Allen

For information about permission to reproduce selections from this book, contact:
Dr. Tiesha Allen
email: theknowledgeumbrella@gmail.com

Book: Harmony Elementary:
Jayla and Hunter's PBIS Tier I Takeover

Written & Illustrated by: Dr. Tiesha Allen

Printed in the United States of America

Harmony
Historians
Harmony
Historians
Harmony
Historians
HARMONY
ROBOTICS
TEAM

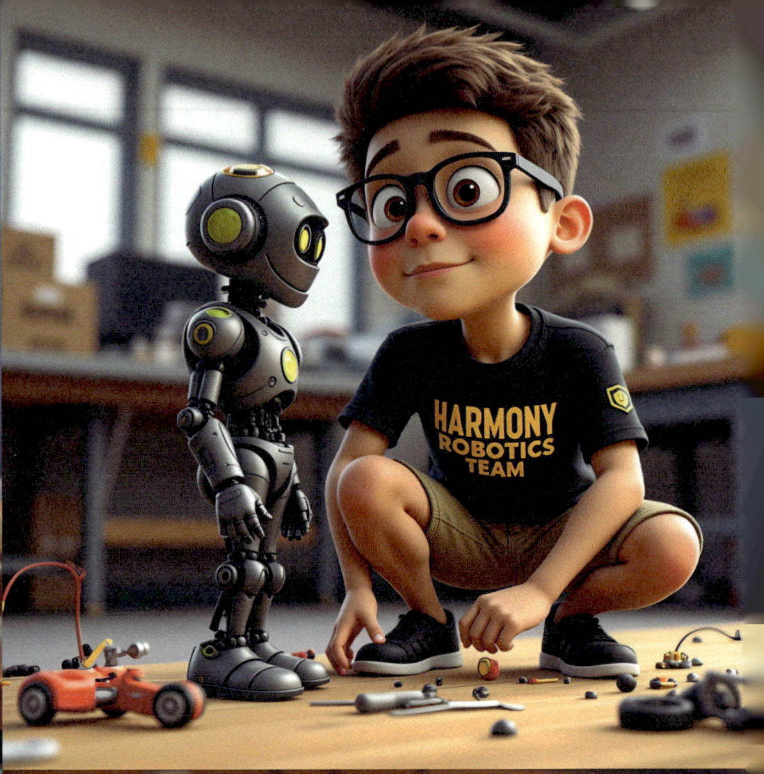

HARMONY
4

Meet Jayla and Hunter

Hi! I'm Jayla, and I'm in the 5th grade at Harmony Elementary. I love history, drawing comic strips, and helping my friends. This year, something awesome happened. I joined our school's PBIS Team! PBIS stands for Positive Behavioral Interventions and Supports. That's just a fancy way of saying we all work together to make school fun, fair, and safe!

And I'm Hunter, a 3rd grader who's all about robotics, basketball, and making sure new students feel welcome. I joined the PBIS Team too because I wanted to help make our school even better for everybody.

At Harmony, we follow three simple but powerful expectations:
Be Respectful. Be Responsible. Be Safe.

Come with us and we'll show you how PBIS works at our school and how it helps all of us become superstars!

1.1 Teamwork Makes the Dream Work

This year, I got to join our school's PBIS Team! It's not just for teachers, but for kids too. Our team includes our principal, counselor, the lunch lady, teachers, students, and even parents. We work together to make our school better for everyone. We all have a voice, no matter our grade.

1.2 Meetings That Matter

Hey Jayla, don’t leave me out! I joined too! The PBIS Team meets every month. We have agendas and take notes to help us stay on track. We even use charts to check our progress, like how many students are earning PBIS points. We do more than just talk. We make real plans and see them happening all around the school.

Be
Respectful
Use Quiet
Voices
Be
Responsible
Walk on the
Right Side
Be
Safe
Face
Forward

1.3 The BIG 3

Our school has three big expectations: Be Respectful. Be Responsible. Be Safe. They are easy to remember and work everywhere, whether I am in the classroom, hallway, on the bus, or in the cafeteria. These expectations are not just rules. They help our school feel like a team.

Remember: *The number and type of PBIS expectations are up to your team. Make sure they are positively stated and reflect your school's values. Keep the list short, simple, and easy to remember so they can be used in all areas of the school.*

1.4 Learning the Expectations Together

Just like there are lessons for academics, there are lessons for PBIS too! At the start of the year, we went on a tour of the school. Our teachers showed us how to be safe on the stairs, respectful in the lunch line, and responsible with supplies. We practiced the right way to do things, and we even played games to help us learn. PBIS lessons are more than just expectations. They help us know what to do before there is a problem.

HARMONY ELEMENTARY
HOW WE BUZZ TOGETHER

BE RESPECTFUL | **BE RESPONSIBLE** | **BE SAFE**

TEACHER HELPS
(small problems)

First Time Helper
- Teacher gives a gentle reminder
- Learn the right way to do it
- Get a special helper strategy

Second Time Helper
- Teacher gives another reminder
- Practice the right way
- Fill out a thinking sheet
- Teacher calls home to chat
- Take a break or lose privilege

Third & Fourth Helper
- Teacher gives reminder again
- Practice the right behavior
- Fill out thinking sheet
- Take a longer break
- Teacher calls parents

SMALL PROBLEMS	BIG PROBLEMS
Talking at Inappropriate Times	Physical Aggression
Off-Task Behaviors	Verbal Aggression
Classroom Disruptions	Chronic Disrespect
Defiance	Stealing
Teasing	Bullying
Inappropriate Use of Technology	Destruction of Property
Dress Code Violations	Bringing Banned Items

OFFICE HELPS
(BIG PROBLEMS)

First Time Helper
- Principal talks with you
- Principal helps you understand and gives consequence
- Your parents get called

Second Time Helper
- Principal talks with you
- Principal figures out what happened
- Principal gives consequence
- Parents, teacher, and principal meet

Third & Fourth Helper
- Bigger consequences
- Extra help with behavior
- Principal helps teacher too

1.5 What's a BIG Deal?

Sometimes people make mistakes. At our school, teachers use a chart to decide if it’s a little problem or a big one. Talking out of turn? That’s small and handled in class. But fighting? That’s serious and goes to the office. It’s fair, clear, and helps everyone understand what to expect.

Remember: Every classroom has special ways to help bees learn good behavior!
We're all learning to buzz together nicely!

1.6 Fair for Everyone

At Harmony, getting in trouble doesn't mean getting yelled at. The adults try to understand what's going on and help us fix it. Like when I got upset in art class, Mr. Claybourne gave me a break and let me talk about it later. That's what PBIS does! It helps us grow, not just punish.

1.7 Teachers Are Learners Too

It is important to have training on PBIS. The entire staff learn ways to help kids solve problems. They even learn how to spot when a kid might need extra help before things go wrong. Our teachers are always learning new ways to support us, and that’s pretty cool.

1.8 Same Expectations, Every Class

In every class, we have voice level charts, a calm down corner, and a point system. My class has group points, and we earn “PBIS Stars” when we follow routines. Even though our classrooms are different, our teachers all use PBIS. That makes school feel fair no matter where you go.

1.9 Caught Being Great

When we follow the Big 3, we earn PBIS Points! I got one last week for helping a kindergartener named Mattie tie her shoes. On Fridays, we shop at the PBIS Store. I bought a pencil with googly eyes!

But just remember: It's not about prizes. It’s about being noticed for doing the right thing.

1.10 All Staff, All In

Everyone gives out PBIS points, including teachers, lunchroom staff, and even our custodian, Mr. Tim. They all go to meetings and share ideas about what is working and what might need to change. When the whole school works together, we feel supported in every part of the school.

1.11 Families Are In, Too

Families don’t just watch from the sidelines. They help out too. My mom came to PBIS Night and helped make posters about safety. Families help make decisions and share ideas. Parents are always welcome, and when families, teachers, and students all work together, our school becomes an even better place.

1.12 What the Numbers Show

The PBIS Team looks at data like how many office visits we have or where problems happen. One time, they saw kids were arguing at recess, so they added more games and helpers outside. We also got ideas from our student ambassadors. That’s using numbers to make real change.

1.13 Changing What’s Not Working

We used to have big messes in the restroom. Water and paper were everywhere! The team looked at the problem and knew we needed a new system. We decided that restroom monitors make all the difference. After about three weeks, the restroom referrals totally dropped! It feels good to help fix things. PBIS means we solve problems together.

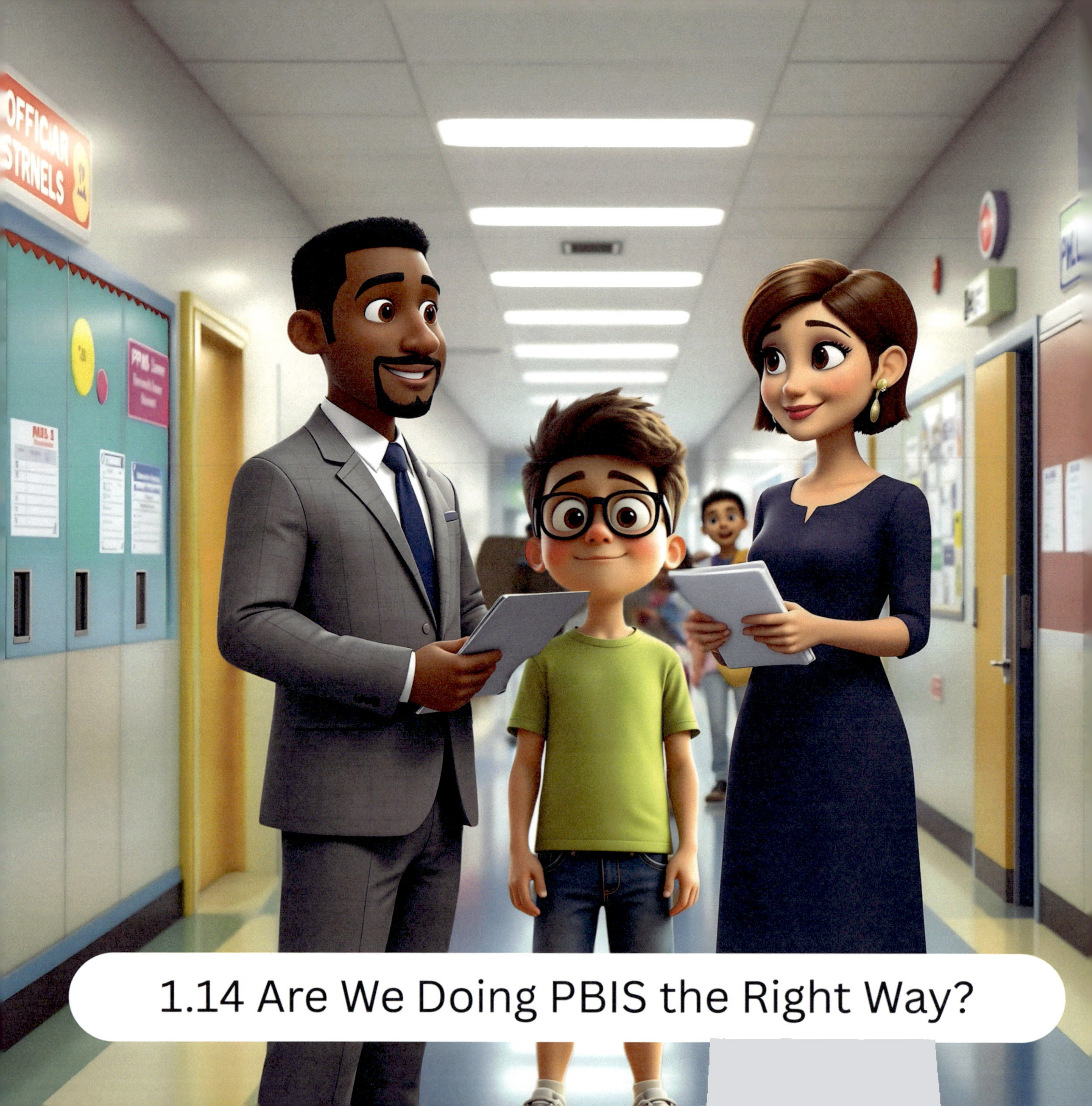

1.14 Are We Doing PBIS the Right Way?

Grown-ups check if PBIS is working the way it’s supposed to. They visit classrooms, look at the point system, and ask us what we think! It’s not about being perfect, but it’s about doing things right and the same across the whole school.

1.15 Time to Celebrate!

At the end of the year, we had a PBIS Glow Party with music, games, and awards! Coach Spincer was even our DJ.

The team showed us how much we improved since last year. We even shared our progress with the community!

PBIS gave us the tools to be leaders, helpers, and Harmony Superstars. We’ve come a long way and we’re proud to be part of it.

Mission Accomplished!

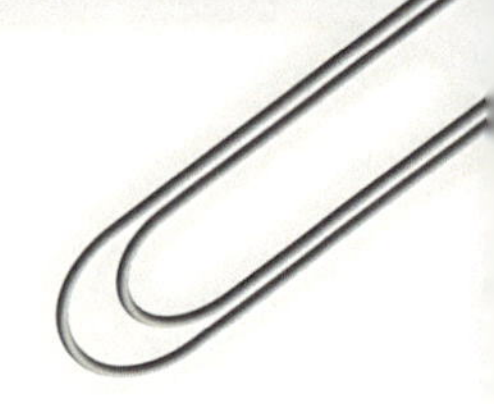

Involve All Staff

Engage teachers, support staff, administrators, and even custodians so everyone understands their role in supporting PBIS.

Use Data to Guide Decisions

Regularly collect and review behavior data to identify trends, celebrate successes, and address problem areas quickly.

Provide Regular Training and Communication

Ensure all staff and students know the expectations and procedures through ongoing training and clear communication.

Recognize and Reinforce Positive Behavior

Consistently acknowledge and reward students who meet expectations to encourage a positive school culture

Be Consistent Across Settings

Make sure expectations and consequences are applied fairly and consistently in classrooms, hallways, cafeteria, buses, and other areas.

Involve Families and Community

Keep families informed and engaged so positive behaviors are reinforced at home and in the community.

Celebrate Successes Together

Share progress and achievements regularly to keep motivation high and remind everyone that PBIS is making a difference.

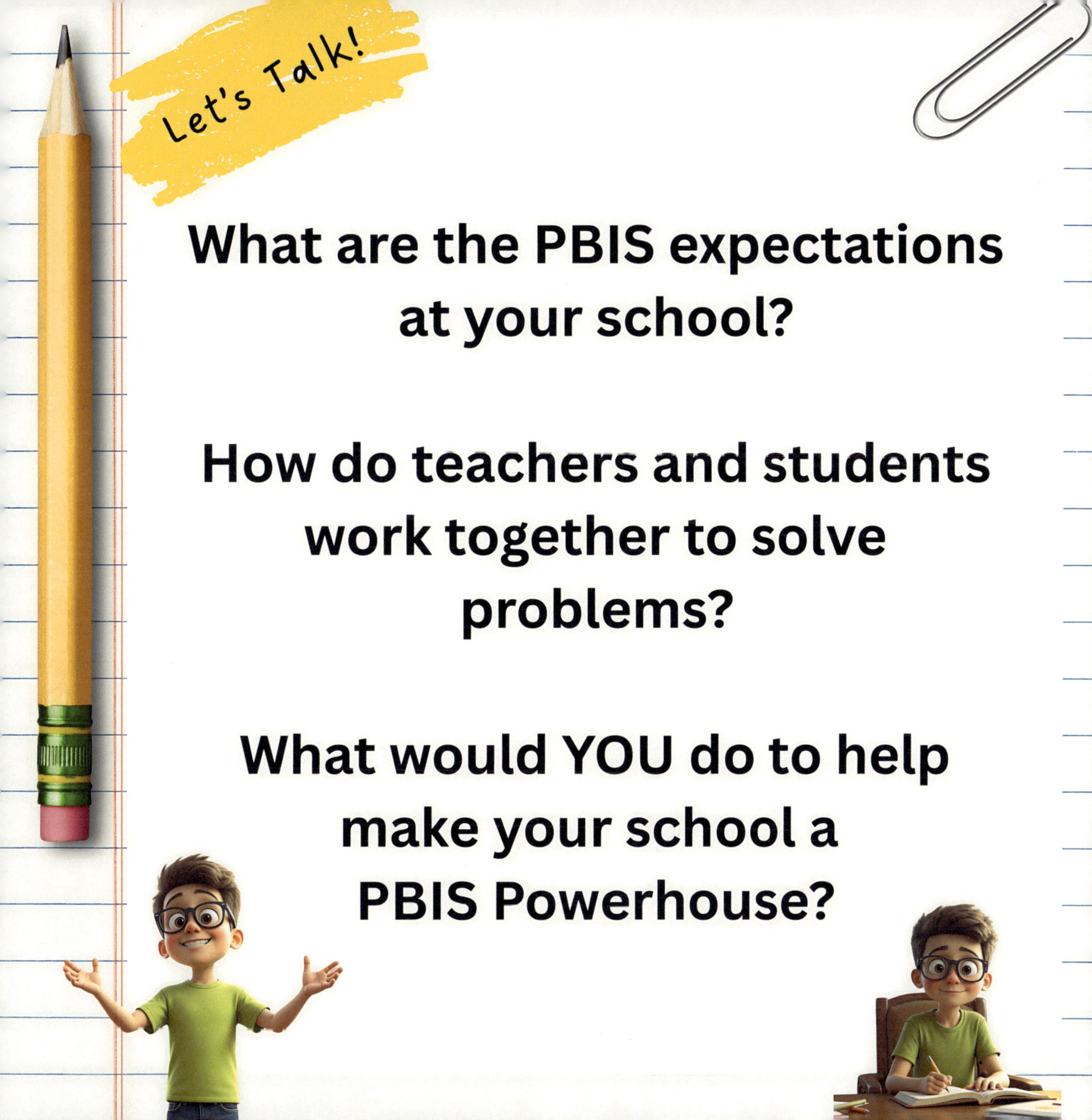
Let's Talk!
What are the PBIS expectations at your school?
How do teachers and students work together to solve problems?
What would YOU do to help make your school a PBIS Powerhouse?

Made in the USA
Columbia, SC
01 August 2025